Igniting Sales
EQ

Igniting Sales EQ

Driving Sales Confidence During Uncertainty

By Lance Tyson

Copyright © 2020 by Lance Tyson.

All rights reserved. No part of this book may be used or reproduced in any manner whatsoever without prior written consent of the author, except as provided by the United States of America copyright law.

Printed in the United States of America.

ISBN: 979-8-669-98647-6

This publication is designed to provide accurate and authoritative information in regard to the subject matter covered. It is sold with the understanding that the publisher is not engaged in rendering legal, accounting, or other professional services. If legal advice or other expert assistance is required, the services of a competent professional person should be sought.

Table of Contents

Acknowledgments 7

Introduction
To Sell is Human 9

Chapter One
It All Begins With Grit 17

Chapter Two
The Choice to Change 25

Chapter Three
Tipping the *Sales* 35

Chapter Four
What Worked Then Won't Work Now 45

Highlights Reel 52

Acknowledgments

"Lance knows sales. He knows there is no magic elixir for successful salespeople because they get ahead by developing and practicing their game. Using the skills he developed over decades in the marketplace, Lance teaches the entire sales continuum from qualifying prospects to overcoming objections to closing the deal. Our company benefitted from Lance's methods and you will too. Read this book and take advantage of Lance's time in the trenches."

- Michael J. Kuntz, Executive Vice President, Turner Construction

"If you combine Lance's thirty years of personal selling experience with the thousands of salespeople he has trained, you can be assured that he has heard and seen every situation you could imagine. When Lance trains, the time flies by because you are learning so much. It's entertaining; he has great energy and a million stories and examples. He has found a way to capture that same essence into the pages of this book. You will laugh and be inspired, all while learning a process that defines successful selling. Thank you, Lance, for taking your knowledge and teachings and sharing them for all to see. You have given those willing to invest in themselves all the necessary tools to go out and carry on highly skilled sales conversations."

- Chad Estis, Executive Vice President, Business Operations, Dallas Cowboys Football Club

Acknowledgments

"Lance Tyson has made a profound and lasting impact on the world of sports business. Lance prepares for a session like no other; he has an uncanny ability to read the environment of a sales team during a session and adjust his content to ensure they get the most out of the day. You, as a manager, will see the benefits of Lance's methods weeks and months after he is gone. I have utilized Lance during my tenures in the NBA, the NFL, and now on the agency side of the business. There is absolutely no one better in the world of behavioral modification, sales training, management training, or developing scalable sales processes that produce world-class results. Proud of you, my friend, and I thank you for all that you have done for me."

- Todd Fleming, Vice President and GM, Legends Global Sales

"We have had the pleasure of working with Lance and Tyson Group for over eight years. I can say, without any hesitation, his training, coaching, and direct approach to the sales process has had an impact with our entire ticket sales and service team. Most importantly, his management training program has helped expand the professional growth within our ticket sales and service leadership team. Lance's passion, team-first attitude, and overall genuine empowering personality allow him to connect at a level with all members of our ticket sales and service team.

- Kevin J. Dart, Vice President of Ticket Sales/Service/Operations, New York Yankees

Introduction

To Sell is Human

LANCE-ISM #77

"SALES HAS NEVER BEEN ABOUT B2B OR B2C... IT'S ABOUT HUMAN TO HUMAN (H2H)."

Introduction: To Sell is Human

Have you ever thought about the potential of a $5 bar of iron? If you've never seen one, there's not much to it. Just a simple rectangle, like a bar of gold bullion, though a heck of a lot less expensive. But just because it's a $5 bar of iron doesn't mean it has to stay that way. There are actually lots of things you can do to increase its value.

If you take that $5 bar of iron and melt it down and turn it into horseshoes, you could more than double its value to $12. Not bad. And if you take that $5 bar of iron and turn it into sewing needles, you increase the value to nearly $3500. Pretty good for a $5 bar of iron, right? But get this: if you take that same bar of iron and turn it into watch springs for the finest Swiss watches, you increase its value to $300,000!

If you're in the sales game during these times of economic uncertainty, you have your work cut out for you. But the good news is you have a bar of iron ready to be shaped. No, I'm not talking about your product or service. Even in a recession, individuals and businesses still have problems that need solutions. And as long as you have a product or service that's efficient and effective, it has the potential to sell.

The bar of iron I'm talking about is your *sales team*.

But to unlock that potential, you need to understand that there are a whole lot of new variables with selling in today's world. Something called COVID-19 changed the rules of the game—maybe not permanently—but for the next decade or so at least. Virtual conferences, limited-capacity sporting events and entertainment venues, online retail, virtual education, video training; new models for our new world are emerging every day. But the bedrock of sales is what it always has been: we sell *human to human*, or what I call H2H.

That is exactly what makes the process so frustrating for people when it comes to business-to-business (B2B) sales—no matter how many times we try to synthesize it, we still find ourselves selling to another human being. One would expect the same with B2B and business-to-customer (B2C) products. Yet every statistic says the opposite of that. For example, Daniel Pink quoted in his book *To Sell is Human*, that while one in nine Americans make their living in sales, the other eight out of nine are involved in some kind of business development role.[1] That's more than any other time in our history.

Take, for instance, the sales teams out there in today's complex world. Despite the amount of marketing automation data that tells us they've actually cut their selling time in half, there are *more* salespeople interacting directly with customers than ever before. It's almost a two-to-one ratio. You would think with all the business intelligence, data, and information out there, there would be *fewer* salespeople. But guess what? I've been hearing that since 1995! Even with the invention of all this technology—the internet, email, marketing automation—there are more salespeople now than there's ever been. You know what that says? That actually says that certain sales are complex enough that you need to have a *human* involved to help in the buying process.

The fact about selling that a lot of salespeople don't get is that it takes place in the buyer's mind. As the salesperson, you have to

---
1 Daniel Pink, *To Sell is Human* (New York: Riverhead Books, 2013).

Introduction: To Sell is Human

determine how much the potential buyer, or the prospect, knows or doesn't know. But how do you unlock a door into a buyer's mind?

With a little key called Emotional Intelligence, colloquially known as *EQ*.

EQ, the psychological equivalent of IQ, is "the capacity for recognizing our own feelings and those of others, for motivating ourselves, and for managing emotions well in ourselves and in our relationships."[2] EQ is an absolute requirement for effective and sustainable relationships, and should not be regarded as a "soft" skill in business, but as a critical one.

When you think about it, buyers actually might have a lot more information than you, or a different version of information. So, you've got to somehow get into their head and enable them to share, so you can help them ultimately weigh out whether the decision's right or not.

If you go back to the late 1800s to John Patterson of the National Cash Register Company (NCR), he invented a new concept called a cash register. At the point of entry, instead of shopkeepers keeping their balances in a ledger, they now could take a customer's money, push certain buttons, and it would tell them how much money they had left over in addition to how much product they had left over. Brilliant, right?

But you have to think about the late 1800s. You've got Nels Olson from *Little House on the Prairie* operating the mercantile out of a cigar box and a ledger book.

Imagine NCR's sales rep riding into Walnut Grove, going up to Mr. Olson and saying, "Hey, Mr. Olson. Do you mind if I ask

---

[2] Daniel Goleman, *Working with Emotional Intelligence* (New York: Bantam Books, 1998).

you how you manage your money?" Mr. Olson pulls out a shotgun. "What the hell are you asking me that for? That's a personal question," says Mr. Olson.

If the sales rep has a high enough EQ, he might leverage it to get into the mind of his buyer, say something like, "Hey, hold on. I've got this concept. If you're like most storekeepers, you probably spend hours a day balancing your books, making sure you're following up on the Ingalls, who are always late and always asking for credit. You're trying to figure out what you have: how much yarn, how many yards of wool, right? I actually have this machine that can save time and be more accurate."

Mr. Olson is intrigued, but skeptical. "What are you talking about? What machine?"

"Well, can I show you?" asks the sales rep.

The sales rep connected with Mr. Olson, related to his needs, and had done enough homework to know that the Ingalls were deadbeats and a pain in the ass to deal with. Then he would train Mr. Olson how to use the cash register. Nels would have it for a couple months, put it on consignment. This guy John Patterson came up with a four-or-five-step sales process, and that's how NCR sold their cash registers. H2H in action.

Let's face it. What's really changed in sales since then? Not much.

Now we communicate over emails, phone calls, Zoom meetings, social media, and text messages in our selling. But it's still H2H selling. That's never going to change. You still have to gain a human being's attention, their interest, see if they're going to be open to a suggestion, dialogue to see if they want it, and then you've got

Introduction: To Sell is Human

to close them. You've got to get them to say yes or no. Maybe is not acceptable. Nothing has changed.

Believe me, I know. I've been a sales professional, entrepreneur, and have trained other salespeople since the 1980s. My experience includes selling vacuums door-to-door in college; leading the largest operation for Dale Carnegie Training outside Taiwan and Hong Kong; building Tyson Group as the go-to salesforce trainers of professional sports teams and insurance organizations; and training over one thousand sales executives and sales managers annually. A who's who of top sports franchises turn to Tyson Group to help their sales teams move to the next level, including:

- Dallas Cowboys
- New York Yankees
- Legends
- Topgolf
- Fenway Sports Management

Even as I write this, we're working with the sales teams of about 60 percent of pro sports organizations. They come to us because we've proven able to rationally assess their sales operations and people, while helping them develop and implement a time-tested H2H sales process.

In this book, I'll lay out the five critical categories of Emotional Intelligence that we teach our clients. And I'll give you my Six Strategies to Igniting Your Sales Team's EQ, so you'll be ready to compete and close at H2H selling in this crazy new world. You and your team will replace counterproductive behaviors with more adaptive action, and build new habits that replace toxic tendencies while improving how others see you, both internally (within teams, across teams, and between departments) and externally (with suppliers, current customers, and prospects).

In times of economic uncertainty and our post-COVID-19 world, igniting the EQ factor in your sales team is more important than ever. The goal of this book is not to help you refine your product or service. If you've made it this far in sales, what you sell is something others need. You just have to convince them they need it. At the end of the day, a sale is simply about selling something that solves a buyer's problem or creates an opportunity. Even in a recession, individuals and businesses still have problems that need solutions. And as long as the product being sold is efficient and effective, your product or service has the potential to sell.

This book is designed to introduce a tried, tested, and proven process for igniting your sales team's EQ factor that will help you sell your goods or services with consistent success. It's a process that will benefit any high performer—from entrepreneur to sales professional to manager trying to boost team performance—and anyone for whom selling is a matter of life and death.

Igniting Sales EQ: Driving Sales Teams' Confidence During Uncertainty redefines sales as you know it. Having a high IQ might get you on *Jeopardy!*, but when it comes to selling, it's just not enough. EQ also matters. In fact, psychologists generally agree that among the ingredients for success in sales, IQ counts for only 10 percent; the rest depends on EQ.[3]

When analyzing star sales performers, it was found that they all had a high EQ, showing emotional competencies to deal effectively with people both outside *and* within their organization.

That means the success of any sales team is dependent upon the people within it working well together—and *Igniting Sales EQ*!

---

3 Michael D. Akers and Grover L. Porter, "Your EQ Skills: Got What It Takes?", Journal of Accountancy. March 2003, https://www.journalofaccountancy.com/issues/2003/mar/youreqskillsgotwhatittakes.

CHAPTER

It All Begins With Grit

> **SELLING IS MORE THAN JUST SAYING AND PRAYING.**

Chapter One: It All Begins With Grit

Mike Ondrejko is the President of Global Sales for Legends, a premium experiences company that specializes in delivering unique and custom solutions in naming rights, sponsorship, premium ticket sales, fundraising, conferences, events, and tours for iconic facilities including SoFi Stadium, Notre Dame, Las Vegas Raiders, Ohio State University, Columbus Crew SC, One World Observatory, and the Rose Bowl. Mike has helped Legends triple in size and expand to include global clients and a full-service sponsorship team. Since 2013, he's led the Global Sales team to secure over $1 billion in strategic partnership deals and premium ticket sales revenue.

Pretty impressive, right? But don't think getting to this level of sales success came easy. Nothing worth doing ever does. Mike got to where he is today because of what all high EQ salespeople have—grit.

After spending some time in sales leadership positions in the mid-2000s at companies like Palace Sports and Entertainment, which owned the Detroit Pistons, and the Cleveland Cavaliers during LeBron James' heyday, Mike was offered a position as the Senior Vice President of Corporate Hospitality for arguably one of the largest entertainment venues in the world—Madison Square Garden (MSG). For the uninitiated, it just doesn't get any bigger than MSG when it comes to sports and entertainment. Though they host the Knicks and the Rangers, they are essentially a full-blown media organization, with an entire division devoted to on stage entertainment.

Mike had to go from zero to sixty—from the mom and pop set-up of a traditional sports team to a large, publicly traded, matrixed organization, where the sports team itself is just one of many priorities. Oh, and they were about to embark on a billion-dollar renovation project.

Now to put this in context, up to that point in time, MSG wasn't used to having to sell anything. For them, bringing in clients was like flipping a light switch. But Mike wanted to introduce some new products and services that related to the renovation, which was going to take some serious selling.

Mind you, he was used to having one conversation, watching the head nod, then going off into the sunset with his idea. Now he had to be smart enough to figure out how to communicate an idea across several different divisions, several different layers of leadership, to get everybody to buy in. Needless to say, he had no playbook. What he wanted to do had never been done. So, what did he do? He asked a lot of questions. He found internal advocates and coaches to use as sounding boards: "How does this work? Why is this happening in this way? I need to figure out how this operates."

He also knew he needed to shield his team from all the layers of management, so they didn't get discouraged. He wanted them to have all the encouragement, tools, coaching, and guidance they needed to go out and execute, with no distractions. And so, he ended up building an awesome sales team at MSG from the ground up, armed with a powerful combination of skill and attitude.

Let's push pause on Mike's story for a moment to break down the difference between a skill (Technical Competence), and an attitude (Emotional Competence).

Chapter One: It All Begins With Grit

First of all, both of these competencies are necessary for success in business. But Technical Competence is an "expected" quality within a job—a necessary skill. It's not usually an optional attribute for a person who has to complete a task or perform a role within the organization. Technical Competence allows you to get to the starting line in terms of dealing with customers, colleagues, and suppliers.

Emotional Competence on the other hand is the ability to read, understand, and interact with people. It's a major component of EQ, and provides the undercurrent of a can-do attitude, a likeable personality, and ultimately what makes the difference in not just H2H selling, but *all* relationships long term. However, this emotional competence tends to be somewhat undervalued in many of today's organizations.

One of the best ways for organizations to reframe Emotional Competency within their sales team is to consider their company as a series of assets being employed to achieve objectives. When we look at any organization in terms of the assets it leverages to succeed, we see that there are various types of assets that need to be considered:

Traditional Assets

- Facilities
- Equipment
- Patents
- Processes

Knowledge Capital

- Who knows what

Emotional Capital

- Feelings
- Beliefs / Values
- Perceptions

When you think about it, the Traditional Assets are only of any real value if they can be used or applied by the organization in the business process. The same thing with Knowledge Capital. It can only be of any real value when it's applied or used by the organization in the form of secrets, knacks, formulae, know-how, IP, or patents to name a few.

Emotional Capital, however, has both internal and external perspectives. The internal—feelings, beliefs, visions—allow traditional assets and knowledge capital to be leveraged. While the external—brand value and goodwill—ensures demand for and use of the products or services generated by the organization; the heartbeat of H2H selling!

The management of the complex relationships between an organization's "assets" can be influenced by the interpersonal interactions between the staff *within* the organization. A focus on Emotional Competency creates a work environment and culture of superior listening skills, questioning skills, ability to give instruction, ability to give and receive constructive feedback, empathy, and knowledge of self.

Mike had all this and more. Plus, a healthy dose of what Angela Duckworth calls "Grit" in her book *Grit: The Power of Passion and Perseverance*. It goes by other names as well. In a 1940 address to life insurance agents, Albert E.N. Gray called it: "The common denominator of success—the secret of every man who has ever been successful—the habit of doing things that failures don't like to do."[4]

Mike's grit would come into play when, unexpectedly, the billion-dollar Madison Square Garden renovation project was

---

4 Albert E.N. Gray, "The Common Denominator of Success" (speech, 1940), Amnesta, http://www.amnesta.net/mba/thecommondenominatorofsuccess-albertengray.pdf.

Chapter One: It All Begins With Grit

delayed. Not a couple of days or a couple of weeks. This delay was a whole *year*.

Talk about sucking the air out of the room. That meant all the sales reps who busted their butts getting commitments weren't going to get those big commissions just yet. And all of the brands who already committed were now going to be told to wait, with Mike and his team praying they didn't get turned off and walk.

Mike had to harness some serious grit, not to mention his high EQ, to ride out this storm. He knew his number one priority was to protect his team. "Yeah, this sucks," he told them, "but now our job is to make sure that we're in position to tell our clients and our partners exactly what's happening. We need to be transparent, truthful, and confident."

As for his clients, he knew he needed to look at the long game. There was certainly a way that he could have squeezed a couple more pennies out of them for the year based on contractual language. But if he treated them fairly and focused on the long-term relationship, it would eventually pay off. At least he hoped. A year later, the renovation projects were back up and running, construction was happening everywhere, asbestos was falling, and the clients-in-waiting were excited to get things rolling.

And then the financial meltdown of the late 2000s hit.

A one-two punch to Mike and his sales team because many of the clients happened to be financial institutions that relied on Troubled Asset Relief Program (TARP) funds to survive. This meant they couldn't spend taxpayer money on internal services that could be seen as "excessive." I know a lot of sales leaders who would have thrown in the towel by then. But not Mike Ondrejko. He knew, as the saying goes, that tough times don't last; tough people do.

He needed to redefine what success meant. Instead of the black and white world where anything less than a sale was a fail, now success was to be found in every lead. Every call taken. Every meeting set. Every advancement of a relationship. And guess what happened?

The very day the TARP funds were paid back by the financial institutions, his phone rang. And rang. And rang. All the clients came running back. They now had money, and they wanted to spend it with a partner they trusted and who respected their position.

Mike looks back on that scenario and says it was the best learning environment that he's ever been in. And he went on to secure over $450 million in suite commitments to help fund the ongoing transformation of MSG, in addition to developing sales and marking strategies to engage C-level leaders.

And today, in case you're wondering, I count Mike among my closest friends. "A smooth sea has never made a skilled sailor," he told me once. "There are so many variables out there that we just have no control over. When it comes to sales, we've got to become masters in sailing through the tough times while maintaining a tolerance for ambiguity. When you have a high EQ, the right answer does not matter. People with high IQs just don't make it within our organization. They might be the smartest person in the room, but if they can't figure out how to get the masses to buy in, it just doesn't matter. If you're a salesperson, you're going to have a script. You're going to have the 10,000 hours of training, prep, and phone calls. But for all the right deals, when you're sitting in that room, you're going to have decisions to make that don't exist in any of those playbooks. Decisions that don't exist in the prior 10,000 hours of training, prep, or phone calls. At the end of the day, you've got to trust yourself to make decisions."

Chapter One: It All Begins With Grit

That's Mike. I would have expected him to do just what he's done. It's that kind of grit, that kind of endurance, persistence, and perseverance that high EQ salespeople have.

And I'd say that's why so many sports teams connect with my process, because at its heart is the kind of grit it takes to win championship games. I'm competitive by nature, so I understand the kind of challenges involved, the perseverance required to close business and compete in a complex world, but only if you have the right process and a high EQ.

It's really about how you define and see yourself, that grit and persistence. Sales ain't easy. It's hard. You need to understand how attitude drives success, as it did for Mike, and how difficult it is to develop the right attitude. You also need to understand the difficult market environment sales professionals face today, regardless of attitude, so you can see for yourself why you need a predictable, proven sales process.

You can coach all day long for skills, and you can always pick up knowledge. But the piece Mike has, that attitude and grit, is something crucial someone has to pull from deep inside themselves.

Be like Mike. Ignite your sales EQ.

CHAPTER

The Choice to Change

> **SOMETIMES KNOWING WHAT WE'RE MADE OF DOESN'T REVEAL ITSELF UNTIL WE'RE FACED WITH A CHALLENGE.**

Chapter Two: The Choice to Change

In 2002, I had the opportunity to buy the Cleveland marketplace of Dale Carnegie franchises. Nine months after that, I bought Columbus. A year later, Cincinnati. By early 2005, we had purchased Indianapolis and had become the largest Dale Carnegie operation in the world outside Taiwan.

At that time, Tyson Group's current VP of Sales, Allison Schuller, was just starting out and worked as an account executive out of our Columbus headquarters. Her boss back then was our VP of Sales, Traci Tigue, who was just a powerhouse at closing deals.

In 2010, we sold our operations and formed an organization called PRSPX, pronounced "prospects." This new organization specialized in the acceleration of the lead generation process for complex sales processes found in industries such as sports, insurance, and technology. We also trained and coached these clients.

Through the transition, Allison maintained her position as an account executive, and reported directly to Traci. Business rolled steadily along, and then Traci got pregnant. For the next several weeks, Allison and the other account executives kept selling, while Traci continued to coach and mentor from afar as she was only coming into the office a couple of days each week. Needless to say, everyone was getting a little nervous in anticipation of Traci's absence for maternity leave. After all, she was a major contributor to the bottom line of the business. She had her own pipeline and was selling like a mad woman. She was involved in all of our deals. She was the closer, like a sniper. The rest of the team would get a really complex deal so far, and then we'd bring in Traci.

As Traci got closer to her due date, Allison took on extra responsibilities where she wasn't just selling new accounts. She was also managing two or three existing clients and handling all the day-to-day communication. And then Traci's pregnancy got to the point where she could no longer start coming down to the office anymore. So, she left for maternity leave, which created a massive void in our team—and also an opportunity. Allison knew that the team needed someone to take the reins, so she decided that she was going to kick ass and takes names for the three months that Tracy would be out of commission.

Now at that point in Allison's career, she admits that she was still pretty immature—very opinionated and not afraid to say what was on her mind. Which is a great quality, but delivery is everything in sales when it comes to prospects, clients, and team members. Deep down, however, she was incredibly driven, super-smart, had a thirst for knowledge, and was always looking to prove and *improve* herself. Granted she had some success by that point, but because of her attitude, people's perception of her capability was pretty limited. And their trust to throw her in front of a decision maker was fragile at best.

Allison's own perception of herself was limited as well. She thought she knew what she knew, but didn't realize there was more to know. For example, as a team lead, she knew how to set tasks and enforce deliverables, but hadn't yet learned how to inspire others. Yet she was so open and determined to learn (high EQ!), she started to figure out what she didn't know about selling, and about leading.

Traci gave birth to her son, Brodie, in May of 2015. And when she came back from maternity leave to find that Allison had been rocking it, Traci couldn't believe her eyes. With two awesome

Chapter Two: The Choice to Change

salespeople, it seemed we were going to be firing on all cylinders at that point.

Three weeks later, tragedy struck.

I got a call one day that there was something wrong with Traci's baby. His liver wasn't functioning. His organs were starting to shut down. The diagnosis from the Cleveland Clinic: biliary atresia, a rare disease of the bile ducts that only affects 300 babies a year in the United States. It was devastating for all of us.

There was a desperate search going on for a liver donor for little Brodie. Hundreds of people volunteered to go in and be tested to see if they could be a donor. Traci was tested as well, and she was found to be a match. But the complication of donating an organ to her newborn meant that she would be out of commission even longer, and she couldn't do any caretaking for her baby.

That's when Allison decided to step up. She wanted to take on more responsibility so that Traci didn't have to worry about anything while she was out. She didn't want *me* to worry about anything while Traci was gone, either. So, in an amazing act of courage, Traci decided that she was going to indeed be the live donor. In October of 2015, just five months after giving birth to Brodie, the two of them underwent surgery, Brodie's lasting twelve and a half hours. Doctors ended up giving the baby 30 percent of Traci's liver, and thank goodness the surgery was a success. In the meantime, we launched a GoFundMe campaign and everything else we could think of from a company perspective to try and support Traci, while the family set up a Facebook page called Brodie's Good Vibe Tribe.

Allison filled the role as the Director of Sales for a little over a year-and-a-half, and she killed it. Meanwhile, Traci had been weighing all of her priorities, and all the changes that had taken place.

Ultimately, she decided that it was best for her and her family if she didn't return to our team. With that decision, Allison knew that she had a little bit more proving to do, but she set a goal for herself that she would learn everything she could to earn the promotion to the VP of Sales before she was thirty.

And that was a goal I was proud to help her hit.

For anyone looking to make a change in themselves like Allison, here's a shock to the system—*you* control *your* behavior. *You* choose how you feel. *You* choose when you are annoyed, stressed, hopeful, motivated, and everything else in between. Essentially, *you* control the development of your EQ! Which means, *you* get to choose to change. This is not to say that other people or situations can influence how you feel and behave. But your actions and reactions are all on you.

And as we all know, our behaviors are critical. After all, when you look at behavior within interpersonal situations, you'll find it will either enhance the interpersonal process through helping to establish rapport or trust through complementing the verbal signals, or damage the interpersonal process through contradicting the verbal signals.

Have you ever wondered why people sometimes form inaccurate impressions about you? Do they rush to judge you too quickly? This limited view we have of ourselves, and of others judging us only on what they see of us is called the Iceberg Effect.

Quite simply, people will size you up and draw their conclusions about you based primarily upon what they see, how you act. Essentially, your EQ. That means how you choose to display yourself to the world will determine how they form an impression of you and how you will be accepted. Or if they want to close a sale with you.

The best salespeople exhibit behavioral activity that matches those that they are dealing with, that go out of their way to make that H2H connection. That's means having a high EQ.

But EQ isn't just one dimension, one aspect of your personality. It's so much more than being nice, opening the door for others, letting your colleagues hit the buffet line first, making someone laugh until they shoot wine out of their nose, or refusing to take the last grape tomato from the salad bar.

EQ is siloed into five distinct categories, and are as follows:

Self-Awareness

The ability to recognize an emotion as it "happens" is the key to your EQ. Developing self-awareness requires tuning in to your true feelings. If you evaluate your emotions, you can manage them. The major elements of self-awareness are:

- Emotional awareness—your ability to recognize your own emotions and their effects
- Self-confidence—sureness about your self-worth and capabilities

Self-Regulation

You often have little control over when you experience emotions. You can, however, have some say in how long an emotion will last by using a number of techniques to alleviate negative emotions such as anger, anxiety, or depression. A few of these techniques include recasting a situation in more positive light, taking a long walk, and meditation or prayer. Self-regulation involves:

- Self-control—managing disruptive impulses
- Trustworthiness—maintaining standards of honesty and integrity
- Conscientiousness—taking responsibility for your own performance
- Adaptability—handling change with flexibility
- Innovation—being open to new ideas

Motivation

To motivate yourself for any achievement requires clear goals and a positive attitude. Although you may have a predisposition to either a positive or negative attitude, you can, with effort and practice, learn to think more positively. If you catch negative thoughts as they occur, you can reframe them in a more positive terms—which will help you achieve your goals. Motivation is made up of:

- Achievement drive—your constant striving to improve or to meet a standard of excellence
- Commitment—aligning with the goals of the group or organization
- Initiative—readying yourself to act on opportunities
- Optimism—pursuing goals persistently despite obstacles and setbacks

Empathy

The ability to recognize how people feel is important to success in your life and career. The more skillful you are at discerning the feelings behind others' signals, the better you can control the signals you send them. An empathetic person excels at:

- Service Orientation—anticipating, recognizing, and meeting clients' needs
- Developing Others—sensing what others need to progress and bolstering their abilities
- Leveraging Diversity—cultivating opportunities through diverse people
- Political Awareness—reading a group's emotional currents and power relationships
- Understanding Others—discerning the feelings behind the needs and wants of others

Social Skills

The development of good interpersonal skills is tantamount to success in your life and career. In today's always-connected world, everyone has immediate access to technical knowledge. Thus, "people skills" are even more important now because you must possess a high EQ to better understand, empathize, and negotiate with others in a global economy. Among the most useful skills are:

- Influence—wielding effective persuasion tactics
- Communication—sending clear messages
- Leadership—inspiring and guiding groups and people
- Change Catalyst—initiating or managing change
- Conflict Management—understanding, negotiating, and resolving disagreements
- Building Bonds—nurturing instrumental relationships
- Collaboration and Cooperation—working with others toward shared goals
- Team Capabilities—creating group synergy in pursuing collective goals

Raising your EQ to be able to compete and close deals in a complex world is an effort you have to make. You must have that common denominator of results-driven grit for success. You have to persevere. The sales profession is so difficult. You get your ass kicked on a day-to-day basis. People say no to you nine times out of ten. People lie to you and act like your friend, then dodge your calls. If you don't have true sales grit like Mike Ondrejko, at the end of the day, you're going to get your ass kicked. And if you don't understand the power of EQ and work to ignite it, then that will kick your ass, too.

CHAPTER

Tipping the *Sales*

> **YOU CAN'T WIN IF YOU CAN'T SCORE."**

Chapter Three: Tipping the *Sales*

For years, early in my career, I had done a lot of work with casinos. In doing some business with the Detroit Red Wings, I got to stay at Motor City Casino, which are both owned by members of the Ilitch family. I was talking to the general manager there, and he filled me in on how a casino logistically tips the scales in its favor by appealing to those with a lower EQ. The fact is, a casino makes money at a higher percentage on some games than others. There's no secret to that. If you think about how Vegas is set up, or any casino for that matter, the game they really want you to play is slots, the one-armed bandit. They want you to play the slot machines because the odds are better for the house. If you go to a casino floor, you'll find they actually route you through multiple layers of slots. In the grand scheme of things, what are your odds, really, on slots? Who are the odds in favor of?

They're more in the house's favor. The barrier to entry for slot machines is low. They're loud and flashy and draw you in. You push a button and pull a lever. If you think about it, people like to play slots because it's not hard. You stick your card in, push a button, and pull a lever.

But if you made your way through the layers of slots, where do they start routing you? Where do the layers go? Well, if you went fifty feet up in the air, you'd see they start routing you to something a lot of people play: card games. The next game they want you to play is poker or blackjack, because the odds are still a little bit more in the favor of the house. And most people with an average EQ have been taught to play cards at some point, so there's a comfort level there.

The game beyond that is roulette. This is where the scales start to tip a little less toward the house and more toward the player. You'll notice on the casino floor tour that there are a hell of a lot fewer roulette wheels than there are slot machines.

Then come the games that are furthest out, the hardest to access as a player: keno and craps. If you look at your odds, if you do any research, your odds as a player are some of the best with craps. Typically, though, you have six to eight craps tables in a 24-hour casino. On average, probably three are being played at any one time. You have layers of what your lowest bet is. But if you pull up to a craps table and you start watching the game, you'll find it intimidating. Why is it intimidating? Well, you have ten to twelve people standing around the table, yelling and throwing things. There are distractions, and one person has the dice, but everybody's playing. They're high-fiving each other, and they're yelling about nine different bets out that seem very complex. But if you take the time to understand the game a little bit, you'll find they're not that complex.

Then you roll the dice and you say silly stuff like, "Mama needs a new pair of shoes." I remember I said that in front of my brother one time, and I won at craps. He said, "Mama? Who the hell calls Mom, *Mama*?"

It's all very distracting, kind of like today's marketplace, where you have social media and people's opinions and reviews and the like. But craps really isn't that hard once you make your way back to those tables. And your odds of beating the house are better if you learn to play it.

Chapter Three: Tipping the *Sales*

The same concept applies to selling. Salespeople need to keep it simple and learn the process of leveraging their EQ so they can start to tip the scales in *their* favor. Because let's face it, just like a casino, the sales odds are in the buyer's favor. When someone is interested in buying something, they are going to be concerned about how much things cost, whether their opinion will be taken into account, and if they even have the time to listen. Plus, the buyer is going to be armed with more information than they would have been in the past through the power of the internet, which is going to make them a lot more confident than they once were.

You need to have a strategy that takes into account all of those pieces of the buyer's mind-set. It has to be flexible enough that you can tailor it to individual clients, but sturdy enough that it can be scalable and repeatable. You have to have a predictable way to sell.

You're going to think in terms of: If this, then that. If I get someone's voicemail, what do I say? How do I deal with an objection about price? How do I give my Impact Statement? How do I present things in a logical fashion?

You're also going to develop skills that apply in any process: things like verbal brevity, resolving objections, being able to facilitate, and selling over the phone versus selling in person. Remember, the sales process is simply the buying process in reverse.

Think about the steps you take when you buy something, a pair of sneakers, for instance. Something in your world gets your attention and you come to the conclusion: I need a new pair of sneakers. You start to go out and look, try a couple pairs on, go to the store, go to Amazon.com. In that process, you remove doubt, because you're actively looking. Then you start to consider it, lay it out and say, "Jeez, do I really need these? What pair do I need?" Ultimately, you buy a pair. That's a simple buying process.

In most sales, especially B2B sales, it's more complex. You take action to get somebody's attention. You need to qualify them to see if they would fit business parameters. You have to engage the prospect in some kind of request for their time, ask them a series of questions that are really for their benefit, and get the buyer in a scenario where you can present them with an idea in order to start creating an opportunity where one did not exist before. Then you present something that removes their doubt, and gets them saying, "This is a decent fit for me." Finally, you get into dialogue with them to remove any objection and close.

You're just inverting the buying process by taking every action that somebody would normally take when they buy something. That's the essence of the job, and the essence of H2H selling.

It's not the kind of situation you will solve with the force of your personality, no matter how charismatic a salesperson you are. You need a predictable process to get in alignment with what's in the buyer's mind.

And to do that, you need my Six Steps to Igniting Your Sales Team's EQ:

1. Positive Mindset and Self-Talk

Self-talk has a major impact on your mindset. Your mind-set has a major impact on how you will interact with other people. Self-talk can cause your behavior to reflect what you expect to happen rather than what you want to happen. Keep in mind:

- Positive self-talk leads to a positive outcome
- Negative self-talk leads to a negative outcome

2. Turn Self-Deception into Self-Awareness

Personality, and thereby EQ, is composed of two parts: 1) Identity or how we see ourselves, and 2) Reputation or how others see us. For most people, there is a disparity between identity and reputation that can cause them to ignore feedback and derail their efforts. Real self-awareness is about achieving a realistic view of one's strengths and weaknesses, and of how those strengths and weaknesses compare to others'. For instance, most people rate their own EQ highly, yet only a minority of those individuals will be rated as emotionally intelligent by others. Turning self-deception into self-awareness will not happen without accurate feedback, the kind that comes from data-based assessments such as a valid personality tests or 360-degree feedback surveys. Such tools are fundamental to help us uncover EQ-related blind spots, mostly because other people are generally too polite to give us constructive feedback.

3. Turn Self-Focus into Other-Focus

Paying due attention to others is tantamount to career success. But for those with lower levels of EQ, it's difficult to see things from others' perspectives, especially when there is no clear right or wrong way forward. Developing an other-centric approach starts with a basic appreciation and acknowledgement of team members' individual strengths, weaknesses, and beliefs. Brief but frequent discussions with team members will lead to a more thorough understanding of how to motive and influence others. Such conversations should inspire ways to create opportunities for collaboration, teamwork, and external networking.

4. Be More Rewarding to Deal With

People who are more employable and successful in their career tend to be seen as more rewarding to deal with. Rewarding people tend to be cooperative, friendly, trusting, and unselfish. Unrewarding individuals on the other hand tend to be more guarded and critical. They are willing to speak their minds and disagree openly but can develop a reputation for being argumentative, pessimistic, and confrontational. Although this reputation helps enforce high standards, it's only a matter of time before it erodes relationships and the support for initiatives that accompany them. It's important that these individuals ensure an appropriate level of interpersonal contact before tasking someone or asking them for help. Proactively and frequently sharing knowledge and resources without an expectation for reciprocity will go a long way.

5. Control Your Temper Tantrums

Seriously, you're not three-years-old anymore. Passion and intense enthusiasm can easily cross the line to become moodiness and outright excitability when the pressure's on. Nobody likes a crybaby. And in the business world, those who become particularly disappointed or discouraged when unanticipated issues arise are viewed as undeserving of a seat at the grown-ups' table. If you're one of many people who suffer from too much emotional transparency, reflect on which situations tend to trigger feelings of anger or frustration. Monitor your tendency to overreact in the face of setbacks. For example, if you wake up to a bunch of annoying emails, don't respond immediately. Wait until you have time to calm down. Likewise, if someone makes an irritating comment during a meeting, control your reaction, and keep calm. While you can't exactly go from being Woody Allen to the Dalai Lama, you can avoid stressful situations and inhibit your volatile reactions by being aware of your triggers. Start working on tactics that help you become aware of your emotions in real time, not only in terms of how you experience them, but more importantly, in terms of how they are being experienced by others.

6. Display Humility, Even if it's Fake

Why? Because fake humility in sales is better than no humility at all. I get it, sometimes it can feel like you're working on an island managed by six-year-olds. But if you're the type of person who often thinks, "I'm dealing with idiots," then it's likely that prospects will view your self-assured behaviors as arrogant, forceful, and incapable of admitting mistakes. Climbing the organizational ladder requires an extraordinary degree of self-belief, which up to a certain point is seen as inspirational. However, the most-effective leaders are the ones who don't seem to believe their own hype, for they come across as humble. Striking a healthy balance between assertiveness and modesty, demonstrating receptiveness to feedback, and the ability to admit one's mistakes, is one of the most difficult tasks to master. When things go wrong, team members seek confident leadership, but they also hope to be supported and taught with humility as they work to improve the situation. To ignite this component of EQ, it is sometimes necessary to fake confidence, and it's even more important to fake humility. We live in a world that rewards people for hiding their insecurities, but the truth is that it is much more important to hide one's arrogance. That means swallowing one's pride, picking and choosing battles, and looking for opportunities to recognize others even if you feel you are right, and others are wrong.

In sales, we want to be playing craps rather than the slots. We don't have to be gamblers, but we do have to be odds players. Given all the challenges of today's marketplace, we need to learn a thing or two from the casinos. We need to even the odds and tip the scales in our favor… or should I say, tip the *sales* in our favor, by igniting our sales EQ!

CHAPTER 4

What Worked Then Won't Work Now

> **BE YOUR OWN ARCHITECT. THE WORLD IS YOUR OYSTER.**

Chapter Four: What Worked Then Won't Work Now

In the early 2000s in the Atlantic, there was a tense showdown between a Spanish ship and the US Navy. Essentially, there's an emergency frequency that maritime uses, and a message went out from a small Spanish boat to the USS Lincoln, the second largest battleship in the Navy. The Spaniard said, "We need you to adjust your course by 15 degrees North. You're headed right for us." Do you think the United States Navy was going to bow down to a foreign ship? Hell no. The US responded: "No, we need *you* to immediately move 15 degrees South." The captain of the Spanish ship got back on and said, "Look, that is not possible or convenient. We need you to adjust." The Americans response was: "We actually demand that you change your course." Spain responded with: "Sorry, we can't, it's not convenient."

This exchange went back and forth for a while, until finally the US captain picked up the radio and said, "Look, I'm the captain of the USS Lincoln. We're the second largest battleship in the US Navy. We need you to adjust your course very quickly." Again, Spain responded "That's not going to happen." The US Navy replied: "We are accompanied by two battleships, six destroyers, five cruisers, and multiple support craft. We demand that you change your position 15 degrees South." Moments later, the Spanish captain responded: "We're accompanied by a dog, two of us, some provisions, and a Canary that's asleep. We highly suggest you change your course because we're actually on dry land and you're not far out. By the way, we have no clue where we rank in terms of lighthouses on the glacier coast. We know we're part of NATO, but you need to change your course."

The US response? "Okay."

What this story demonstrates at the end of the day is that bullying, intimidation, shaming, guilting—low EQ tactics—doesn't work anymore. What worked then won't work now. Power lies in the ability to connect emotionally. With everything that's happening in the world, the uncertainty in business, the uncertainty in sales, the social climate, the wokeness, H2H selling is more relevant than ever.

But it all comes down to igniting the EQ mindset, especially during times of uncertainty. As I'm writing this book, the world is gripped by COVID-19 and social justice movements that are long overdue. The landscape of *everything* has changed, not just with sales.

We need to have more empathy as human beings. We NEED to change our mindset and ignite our EQ.

I get it, there's a ton of misinformation and uncertainty out there. Do we go or do we wait and see? Do we actually have the right people on the team? Can we sell our way through this? We're training, but training for what? And as many times as I hear people ask, "What's the new normal?" my response is: "There is no new normal. There's a new *business reality*."

In some cases, opportunities are going to be scarce. There are industries that are going to be hunting in winter for a long time. On the flip side, there are also going to be new opportunities. There are going to be new products, new services to offer. This uncertainty is going to require us to sell more creatively, and when you're being creative, you're going to think like a buyer.

There was a book a few years ago called *Blue Ocean Strategy*. The concept was that a blue ocean means that the water is deep, has a lot of fish, and has fewer people fishing. For a lot of us though in

Chapter Four: What Worked Then Won't Work Now

the months and years ahead, business will be in a red ocean; shallow water, fewer fish, more competitive fishing, bloody with competition.

There will be reduced resources to get the job done. Budget constraints might require you to re-work and re-imagine a lot of deals. Marketplace obstacles are going to affect how you do business—shifting priorities, unsolvable objections in some cases, the restrictions imposed by COVID…the list goes on. This pandemic is a 360-degree issue. It's not like Hurricane Katrina that just happened to New Orleans. COVID has happened *everywhere*. It's affected *everybody*. And it's disrupted the very basic levels of Maslow's hierarchy of needs.

So, the landscape has changed. From a sales perspective, this means competition. The pressure is going to be on sales leadership to select the right teams, to draw up the right game plan. And that game plan is going to require igniting their team's sales EQ. Sales leaders and their team are going to need to learn how to think on the fly, to improvise, to get creative. Have you ever wondered how a SEAL team, who *strictly* operates in times of uncertainty, can have an 80 percent success rate? They have an extremely high EQ. Most SEALs teams prepare for seven to eight scenarios prior to a mission, though less than 30 percent of the time do any of those scenarios they prepared for actually happen. Their success is based on great decision-making in the moment.

Like a power play in a hockey game, reading the offense and making the right decision in the moment when you have tilted the odds in your favor is what wins games. In fact, according to a Florida State Sales Institute benchmarking study a few years ago on what it took to be successful in sales, it was determined that the *mindset* to react in the moment was the greatest predictor of success.

When you combine mindset with strategy, skills, and the right tactics, all filtered through the lens of EQ, you *will* succeed in your sales goals.

We have no choice but to become experts at H2H selling—creating rapport and connecting with people. In a rapidly changing marketplace, we need the best odds to be able to do that. That requires igniting sales EQ. People sell to people, and people buy from people. It may sound obvious, but the human being we shake hands with when we strike a deal, virtually or in person, must be someone we connect with on an emotional level.

Remember, rapport is crucial to sales. Rapport, credibility, and understanding the buyer are three sides of the sales outcome triangle. Everything you say and do, even your appearance, adds credibility or detracts from it. Credibility yields trust, and if you have trust, rapport improves. At the same time, you need to demonstrate that you understand the buyer. When those things happen, in equilateral balance, you sell.

Chapter Four: What Worked Then Won't Work Now

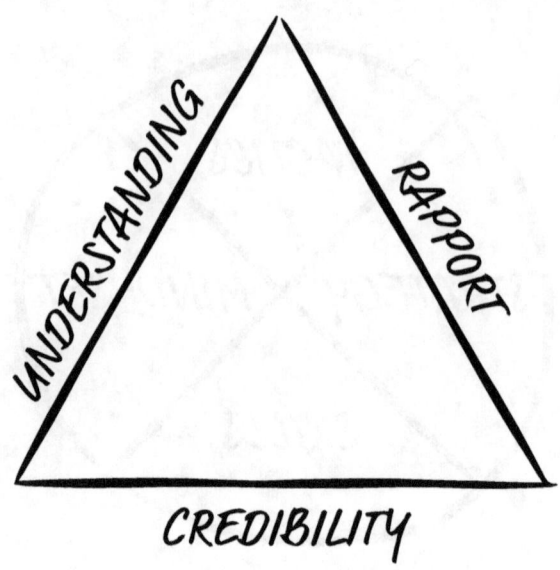

Connecting, however, is the first step toward doing that. It's the step where you overcome preoccupation in the mind of the buyer. You're going to do a much better job at connecting if you remember that it's a two-way street.

Trust me, I know it's a complex challenge to sell in today's marketplace, especially in B2B sales. But there's a simple solution—a process that levels the playing field for salespeople through a step-by-step, replicable strategy that incorporates the tactics needed to win all the battles along the way.

At the end of the day, sales just a series of yeses. "Yes, I'll talk to you. Yes, you can ask me questions. Yes, you can present to me an idea. Yes, you resolved my objection. Yes, I'll buy." It's an algorithm of questions, each followed by five or six yeses. High EQ selling combines creativity with a process for predictable results.

To win the sales game in today's world, you need a mindset adjustment. You need to be willing to learn. You need endurance. You need drive. You need grit.

And you need to Ignite Sales EQ!

HIGHLIGHTS REEL

What factors are at play when people of high IQ fail and those of modest IQ succeed?

Evaluate the ability of people within the organization to work together. What barriers exist and how might they be removed?

Assess your own level of emotional intelligence, that within your department and within the organization overall? Does this have any impact on the performance of the organization?

Which of the Interpersonal Skills, if any, do you consider to be the most important? Why?

Think back to the best communicators you've ever known. Consider why they are successful and how their ability to control the behavior types they display influences others.

www.ingramcontent.com/pod-product-compliance
Lightning Source LLC
Chambersburg PA
CBHW050313220526
45465CB00005B/1974